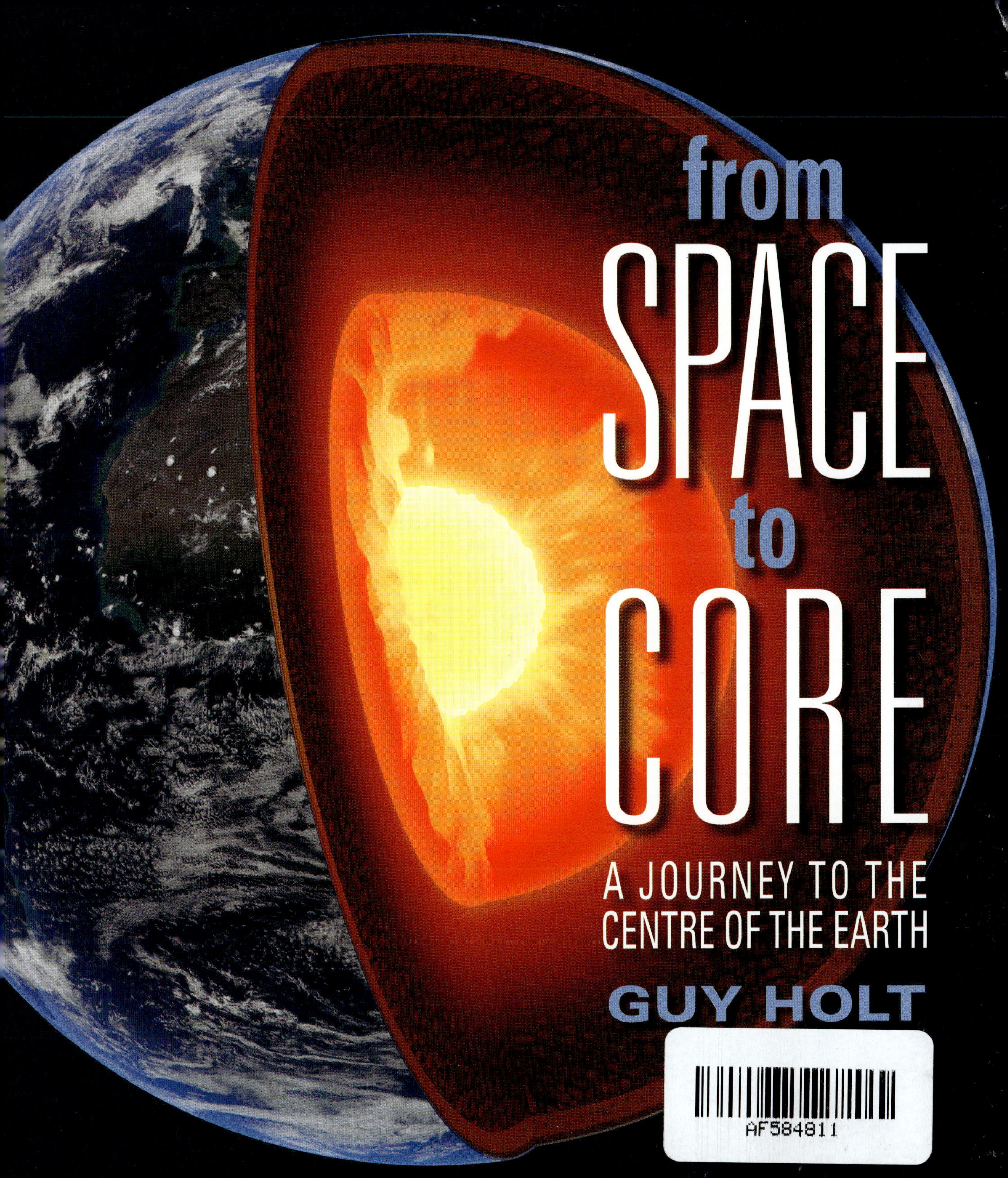

from SPACE to CORE

A JOURNEY TO THE CENTRE OF THE EARTH

GUY HOLT

DID YOU KNOW? Discover interesting and unusual facts with the curious dog Marco

HUMAN-MADE made or produced by human beings rather than occurring naturally

ATMOSPHERIC relating to the atmosphere of the Earth

GEOLOGICAL relating to the Earth's physical structure

FLORA the plants of a particular region or habitat

FAUNA the animals of a particular region or habitat

MARINE relating to or found in the sea

Your journey starts here

The International Space Station

408 km

400,000 m

390,000 m

380,000 m

370,000 m

Largest artificial body in orbit

The International Space Station (ISS) is in low Earth orbit, and makes one complete trip around the Earth in roughly 92 minutes.

- **LAUNCH DATE** 20 NOVEMBER 1998
- **CREW** 6
- **WIDTH** 108.5 metres
- **LENGTH** 72.8 metres
- **SPEED** 27,600 km/h

DID YOU KNOW? The crew's urine is collected and transferred to the water recovery system, where it is recycled into drinking water.

360,000 m

350,000 m

340,000 m

330,000 m

310,000 m

First human to travel into space

Yuri Gagarin was a Soviet pilot and cosmonaut. On 12 April 1961, the *Vostok 1* spacecraft was launched from Baikonur Cosmodrome. He became the first human to travel into space and the first to orbit the Earth.

LAUNCH DATE 12 APRIL 1961
TIME IN SPACE 1 hour and 48 minutes

Yuri Gagarin

327 km

DID YOU KNOW? Gagarin became an international celebrity and was awarded many medals and titles, including Hero of the Soviet Union, the nation's highest honour.

The Space Shuttle

The Space Shuttle program was carried out by the National Aeronautics and Space Administration (NASA). It accomplished routine transportation of Earth-to-orbit crew and cargo from 1981 to 2011. The Space Shuttle was a partially reusable low Earth orbital spacecraft.

FIRST FLIGHT 12 APRIL 1981
CREW 2–7
LENGTH 37.2 metres
SPEED 27,870 km/h
LAST FLIGHT 21 JULY 2011

320 km

DID YOU KNOW? The average cost per Space Shuttle flight was about US$1.5 billion.

The Space Shuttle

300,000 m

290,000 m

The Gravity Field and Steady-State Ocean Circulation Explorer (GOCE)

The GOCE satellite mapped in remarkable detail the Earth's gravity field and the deep structure of the Earth's mantle and hazardous volcanic regions. It also brought new insights into ocean behaviour.

280,000 m

- **LAUNCH DATE** 17 MARCH 2009
- **LAUNCH MASS** 1,077 kg
- **SPEED** 27,870 km/h
- **END OF MISSION** 21 OCT 2013

270,000 m

260,000 m

255 km

250,000 m

DID YOU KNOW? The satellite's arrow shape and fins helped keep the GOCE stable while flying, and flew at a height of 255 kms so it could accurately measure the gravity field.

DID YOU KNOW? *Sputnik* transmitted radio signals back to Earth strong enough to be picked up by amateur radio operators.

230,000 m

223 km

220,000 m

211 km

210,000 m

200,000 m

190,000 m

180,000 m

Sputnik

The first satellite

Sputnik 1 was the first satellite sent into space. It was a polished metal sphere 58 cm in diameter, with four antennas to broadcast radio pulses. It was launched into a low earth elliptical orbit by the Soviet Union. The closest it came to Earth was 223 km, the furthest point from Earth was 939 km.

- **LAUNCH DATE** 4 OCTOBER 1957
- **LAUNCH MASS** 83.6 kg
- **SPEED** 29,000 km/h
- **END OF MISSION** 21 OCT 1957
- **ORBITS COMPLETED** 1,440

LAIKA PRIMUL CALATOR IN COSMOS
1.20 LEI
POSTA R.P.ROMINA

The first spacecraft to carry a living animal

The first living creature (larger than a microbe) to enter orbit was a dog named Laika. She was carried aboard *Sputnik 2* in a padded pressurised cabin. There was just enough room for Laika to lie down or stand. Laika was a street dog, chosen for her toughness.

- **LAUNCH DATE** 3 NOVEMBER 1957
- **LAUNCH MASS** 508 kg
- **SPEED** 7.37 km/s
- **END OF MISSION** 14 APRIL 1958
- **ORBITS COMPLETED** 2,570

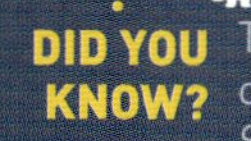

DID YOU KNOW? Ten dogs were considered for the *Sputnick 2* mission. Three where chosen: Laika (the flight animal), Albina (the backup) and Muhka, (for equipment testing).

170,000 m

160,000 m

150,000 m

140,000 m

130,000 m

120,000 m

The Earth's atmosphere consists of five layers that differ in composition, temperature and pressure.

ATMOSPHERE

10,000 km

Exosphere

The exosphere contains hydrogen, helium, carbon dioxide and atomic oxygen.

400 km

Thermosphere

Particles in the thermosphere can have high temperatures because they absorb X-rays and extreme ultraviolet (UV) radiation from the Sun.

90 km

Mesosphere

The mesosphere is the layer where most meteors burn up due to the atmosphere becoming thicker.

50 km

Stratosphere

The stratosphere contains the ozone layer. Most of the ultraviolet radiation from the Sun is absorbed here.

10 km

Troposphere

The troposphere is where the Earth's weather takes place.

SPACE | ATMOSPHERE

110,000 m

112 km

Change of scale

100,000 m

100 km

Kármán Line

The Kármán line is named after Theodore von Kármán, who was the first person to calculate where air becomes too thin for aircraft to fly. This line is used as a boundary to indicate where space begins.

First private space flight

SpaceShipOne was a suborbital spaceplane. Its cabin was designed to hold three people in a short cylinder. The pilot sat towards the front and two passengers could be seated behind. The cabin was pressurised to allow normal breathing.

- **LAUNCH DATE** 20 MAY 2003
- **LAUNCH MASS** 1,092 kg
- **MAX SPEED** 3,518 km/h
- **END OF MISSION** 4 OCTOBER 2004
- **CREW** 1 pilot

DID YOU KNOW? The *SpaceShipOne* could not take off by itself from the ground. It needed a launch aircraft to carry it to launch altitude for an air launch.

99,000 m
98,000 m
97,000 m
96,000 m
95,000 m
94,000 m
93,000 m
92,000 m

BOTTOM OF THE THERMOSPHE

-100°C

90 km

The top boundary of the mesosphere is called the mesopause. This is the coldest part of Earth's atmosphere. Temperatures in this region fall as low as –101°C and vary according to latitude and season.

90,000 m
89,000 m
88,000 m
87,000 m
86,000 m
85,000 m
84,000 m
83,000 m
82,000 m
81,000 m

80 km

80,000 m
79,000 m
78,000 m
77,000 m
76,000 m
75,000 m
74,000 m
73,000 m
72,000 m
71,000 m
70,000 m

Aurora Borealis and *Aurora Australis*

Aurora are natural light displays in the sky. They are most common near the North and South Poles. The lights rays of the Aurora generally reach from 80 km to as high as 640 km above the Earth's surface.

DID YOU KNOW? Aurora are sometimes referred to as polar lights, northern lights (*Aurora Borealis*) or southern lights (*Aurora Australis*).

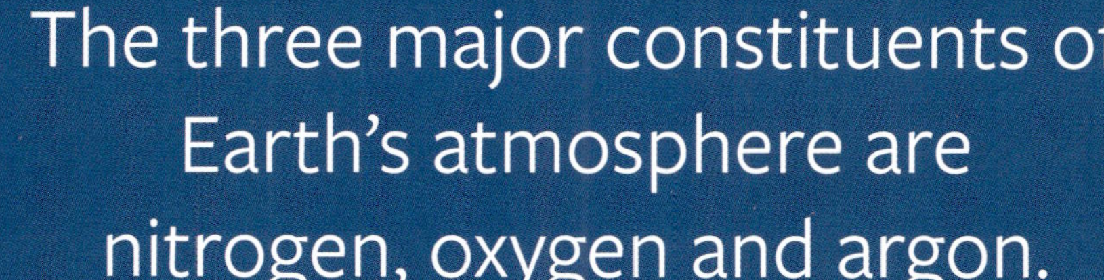

The three major constituents of Earth's atmosphere are nitrogen, oxygen and argon.

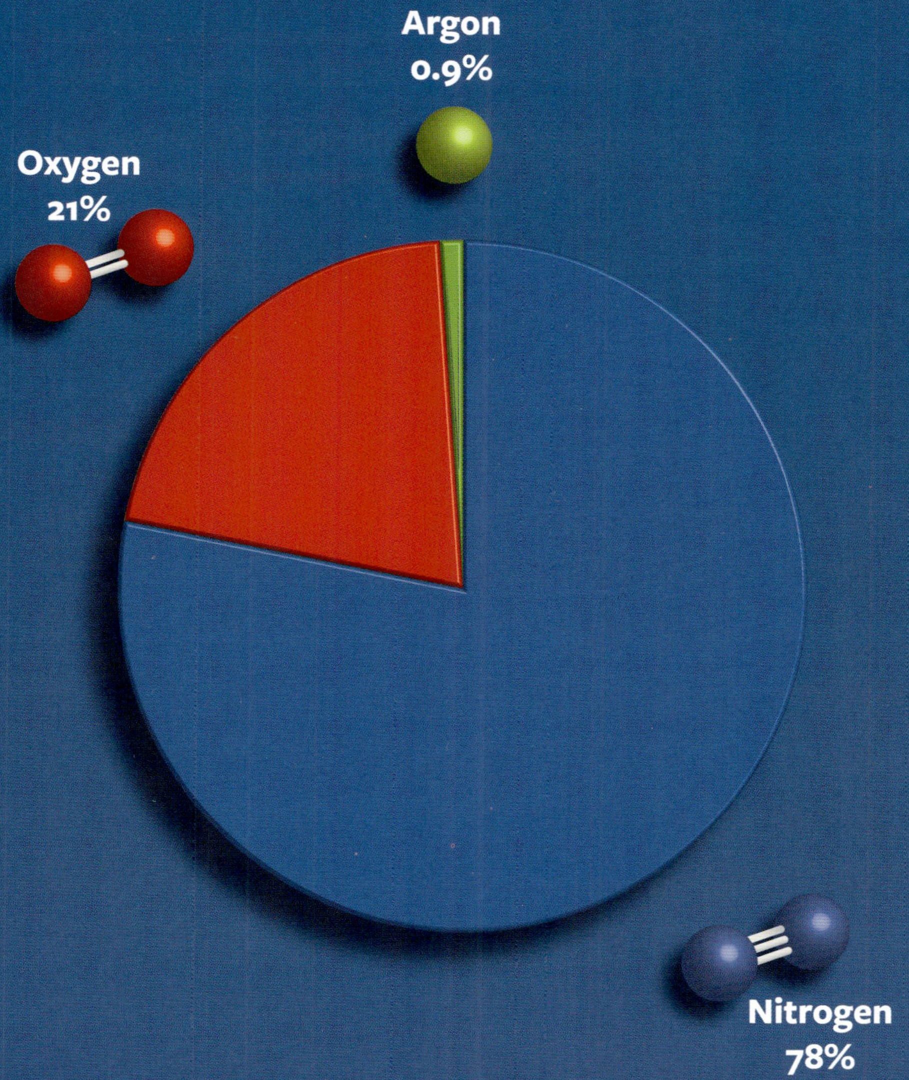

Argon
0.9%

Oxygen
21%

Nitrogen
78%

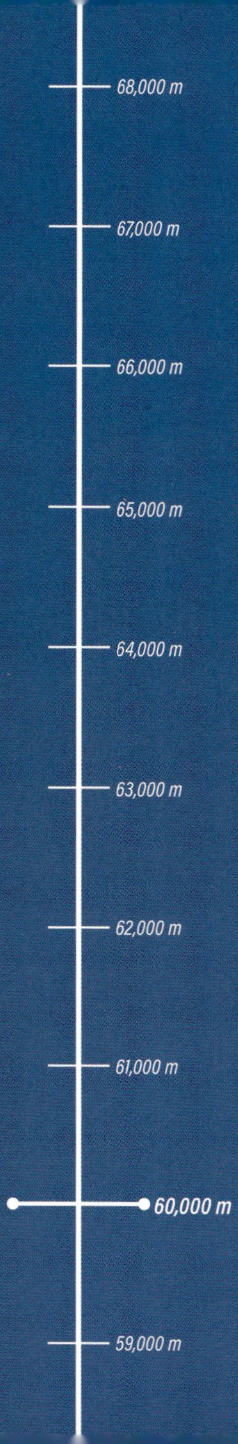

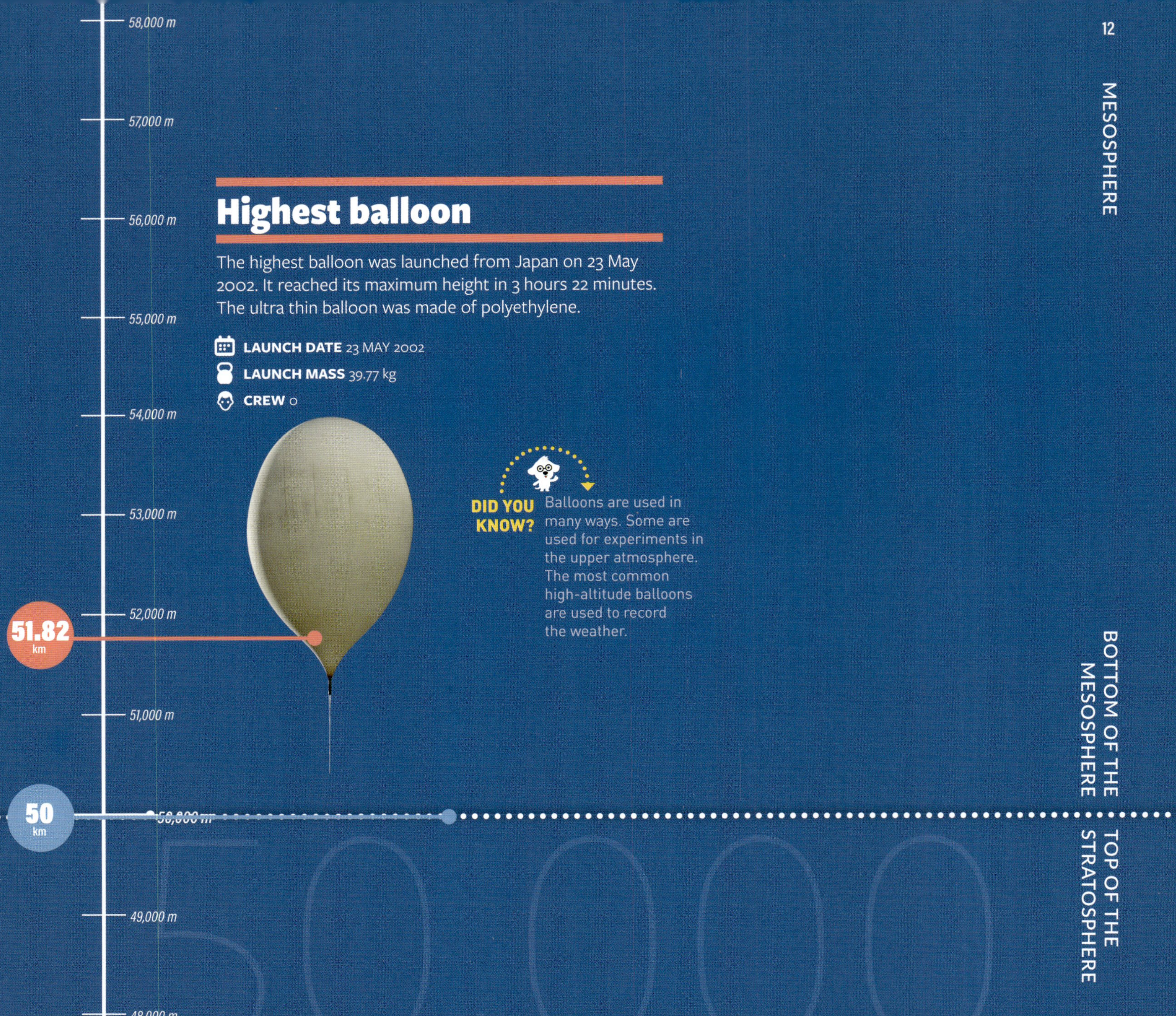

Highest balloon

The highest balloon was launched from Japan on 23 May 2002. It reached its maximum height in 3 hours 22 minutes. The ultra thin balloon was made of polyethylene.

LAUNCH DATE 23 MAY 2002

LAUNCH MASS 39.77 kg

CREW 0

DID YOU KNOW? Balloons are used in many ways. Some are used for experiments in the upper atmosphere. The most common high-altitude balloons are used to record the weather.

46,000 m

45,000 m

44,000 m

43,000 m

42,000 m

41.4 km

41,000 m

40,000 m

39,000 m

38,000 m

37,000 m

Highest altitude freefall jump

On 24 October 2014, Alan Eustace made a jump from the stratosphere. His descent to Earth lasted 15 minutes, setting new world records for the highest freefall jump, and total freefall distance 37,617 metres.

DID YOU KNOW? Alan Eustace is an American computer scientist who served as Senior Vice President of Knowledge at Google.

36,000 m

35 km

Highest altitude paper plane

The highest altitude a paper plane reached was 35,043 metres.

LAUNCH DATE 24 JUNE 2015
LOCATION Elsworth, UK

34,000 m

33,000 m

32,000 m

31,000 m

DID YOU KNOW? The ozone layer was discovered in 1913 by the French physicists Charles Fabry and Henri Buisson.

Exosphere
Thermosphere
Mesosphere
Stratosphere
Ozone layer
Troposphere

Ozone layer

The ozone layer is a region of Earth's stratosphere that absorbs most of the Sun's ultraviolet radiation.

30 km

30,000 m

29.5 km

29,000 m

DID YOU KNOW? *The Helios HP01* was powered by 14 electric engines and was piloted remotely.

Highest propeller-driven aircraft

Helios HP01 set altitude records for propeller-driven aircraft, solar-electric aircraft, and highest altitude in horizontal flight by a winged aircraft.

LAUNCH DATE 8 SEPTEMBER 1999
MAX LAUNCH MASS 600 kg
MAX SPEED 43 km/h
END OF MISSION DECEMBER 2003

28,000 m

26,000 m

25.9 km

24 km

Highest crewed aircraft

The SR-71 was the world's fastest and highest flying operational crewed aircraft. On 28 July 1976 it broke the world altitude record of 25,929 metres.

- **LAUNCH DATE** 28 JULY 1976
- **MAX SPEED** 3,529.6 km/h
- **CREW** 2

23,000 m

Lego-naut

Two Canadian teenagers, launched a Lego-man into space using a weather balloon bought online. It was rigged to a styrofoam box equipped with cameras. The balloon reached its maximum height in about 65 minutes.

22,000 m

21,000 m

20,000 m

20,000

19,000 m

Supersonic airliner

The Concorde was a British–French turbojet-powered supersonic passenger airliner that was operated from 1976 until 2003. It had a maximum speed over twice the speed of sound at Mach 2.04 (2,180 km/h at cruise altitude), with seating for 92 to 128 passengers.

- **FIRST FLIGHT** 2 MARCH 1969
- **EMPTY WEIGHT** 78,700 kg
- **MAX SPEED** 2,140 km/h
- **RETIRED** 24 OCTOBER 2003
- **CREW** 3

18 km

18,000 m

AIR FRANCE

17,000 m

16,000 m

Concorde

15,000 m

DID YOU KNOW? The Concorde's name, meaning "harmony" or "union", was chosen to reflect the cooperation on the project between the United Kingdom and France.

14,000 m

13,000 m

12,000 m

11.8 km

11.3 km

10.9 km

10 km

10,000 m

Change of scale

9.9 km

9,900 m

9,800 m

9,600 m

9,500 m

Highest hang glider

Judy Leden from the UK, gained the altitude record for a balloon-launched hang glider in Jordan on 25 October 1994.

DID YOU KNOW? The earliest forms of gliding originated in China. At the end of the sixth century AD, the Chinese had built aerodynamic kites large enough to carry an average-sized person.

BOTTOM OF THE STRATOSPHERE

TOP OF THE TROPOSPHERE

Highest flying bird

Rüppell's vulture is the highest flying bird, with evidence of a flight at an altitude of 11,300 metres above sea level.

Common crane

The common crane has been recorded flying across the Himalayas. This great height allows them to avoid eagles in the mountain passes.

Commercial aircraft

Commercial airliners fly at altitudes of 10,970–12,500 metres. The Airbus A380 is a four-engine jet airliner and is the world's largest passenger airliner.

DID YOU KNOW? Jet airliners fly at high altitudes because the air is thinner and the engines work more efficiently.

-60°C

Highest paraglider

In 2007, Ewa Wisnierska was trapped in a storm cell and flew to the edge of the troposphere, surviving storm cells, huge hailstones and freezing conditions. Miraculously she survived.

9,300 m

9,200 m

9,100 m

9,000 m

8,900 m

8.84 km

8,800 m

8,700 m

8,600 m

8,500 m

Mount Everest

Highest point on Earth

Measured from sea level, the summit of Mount Everest is the highest point on Earth. It is the fifth-furthest point from the centre of the Earth. Tenzing Norgay and Edmund Hillary made the first official ascent of Everest in 1953, using the south-east ridge route. The Chinese mountaineering team of Wang Fuzhou, Gonpo and Qu Yinhua made the first reported ascent of the peak from the north ridge on 25 May 1960.

DID YOU KNOW? A sherpa named Kami Rita holds the record for most visits to the summit of Mount Everest, which as of 2019 was 24 times.

8,000
8,400 m
8,300 m
8,200 m
8,100 m
8,000 m
7,900 m
7,800 m
7,700 m
7,600 m

Bearded vulture

Bearded vultures are found around or above the treeline. They have been observed living on Mount Everest and flying at a height of 7,300 metres..

Highest active volcano

Nevado Ojos del Salado in the Andes on the Argentina–Chile border is the highest active volcano in the world.

6.4 km

Bar-headed goose

The bar-headed goose is one of the world's highest flying birds. It migrates over the Himalayas to spend the winter in parts of South Asia.

6.1 km

Highest flowering plant

Arenaria bryophylla is a flowering plant that occurs in the Himalayan border regions. It is the highest known flowering plant, occurring as high as 6,180 metres.

6 km

Cirrus clouds

Icy cirrus clouds are thin and do not produce rain. Floating at altitudes of up to 6,000 metres, they often indicate fine weather.

5.6 km

Highest altitude of an insect

In 2008, a colony of bumblebees was discovered on Mount Everest at more than 5,600 metres above sea level, the highest known altitude for an insect.

6,300 m
6,200 m
6,000 m
5,900 m
5,800 m
5,700 m

5.4 km

Highest dwelling animal

Yaks are the highest dwelling domesticated animals on Earth, living at 3,000–5,400 metres.

5.2 km

5.1 km

5 km

5,300 m

Highest settlement

La Rinconada is a city in the Peruvian Andes. It is the highest altitude at which humans live. Its economy is based on the production of gold.

Highest treeline

The treeline of *Polylepis tarapacana* on the extinct volcano Nevado Sajama in Bolivia, is at one of the highest altitudes trees are found on Earth.

5,000 m

4,900 m

4,800 m

Highest railway station

Tanggula (Dangla) railway station is the highest train station on Earth. It is unstaffed and located about 5,000 metres above sea level.

DID YOU KNOW? The location of the station was specially chosen for the view from the platform.

4,700 m

4,600 m

4,500 m

4,400 m
4,300 m
4,200 m
4,100 m
4,000 m
3,900 m
3.8 km
3,700 m
3.65 km
3,600 m

Lake Titicaca

A lake in the Andes on the border of Peru and Bolivia. It is often called the highest navigable lake in the world.

La Paz, Bolivia

At an elevation of roughly 3,650 metres above sea level, La Paz is the highest capital in the world. (It is technically the seat of government, and not the official capital city, which is Sucre.) It sits in a basin surrounded by the high mountains of the Altiplano.

POPULATION 790,000 (2019)

3,400 m
3,300 m
3,200 m
3,100 m
3,000 m
2.85 km
2,900 m
2,800 m
2,700 m
2,600 m

3,000

Quito, Ecuador

Quito is the capital city of Ecuador, and at an elevation of 2,850 metres, it is the second-highest official capital city in the world.

POPULATION 1,848,000 (2019)

10.5°C

DID YOU KNOW? Mid-level clouds sometimes produce virga, which is rain or snow that does not reach the ground.

Mid-level clouds

Found 2,000 metres and above. Often referred to as "alto-" clouds such as altostratus or altocumulus, depending on their shape. Altostratus clouds are flat; altocumulus clouds are puffy. They frequently indicate an approaching storm.

Low-level clouds

Found below 2,000 metres, low-level clouds are also known as stratus clouds. They are often dense, dark, and rainy (or snowy), though they can also be cottony white clumps interspersed with blue sky.

2,400 m
2,300 m
2,200 m
2,100 m
2 km
2,000 m
1,900 m
1,800 m
1,700 m
1,600 m

1.4 km

1,300 m

1,200 m

1,100 m

1,000 m

900 m

800 m

700 m

605 m

600 m

Kathmandu, Nepal

Kathmandu stands at an elevation of approximately 1,400 metres above sea level in the bowl-shaped Kathmandu Valley of central Nepal.

POPULATION 985,000 (2019)

Helicopter

In 1932 two engineers from the Soviet Union managed to get the 1-EA to an unofficial altitude of 605 m, the first successful single-lift-rotor helicopter design ever tested and flown.

Canberra

Canberra is the capital city of Australia. With a population of 420,960, it is Australia's largest inland city.

POPULATION 420,960 (2019)

23.5°C

Hindenburg

The Hindenburg was designed and built by the Zeppelin Company and was operated by the German Zeppelin Airline Company. It flew from March 1936 until it was destroyed by fire 14 months later on 6 May 1937.

- **FIRST FLIGHT** 4 MARCH 1936
- **CREW** 40–61
- **LENGTH** 245 metres
- **SPEED** 135 km/h
- **PASSENGERS** 50–70
- **LAST FLIGHT** 6 May 1937

Seawise Giant

The *Seawise Giant* was the longest ship ever built. Fully laden, its displacement was 657,019 tonnes, the heaviest ship of any kind. It was too large for the English Channel, the Suez Canal and the Panama Canal.

30°C

Sea level

SUNLIGHT ZONE

Freediving record

Herbert Nitsch, an Austrian freediver, is the current freediving world record champion and "the deepest man on Earth" with a world record dive in June 2012 to 253.2 metres.

Giant spider crab

The largest arthropods on Earth, giant spider crabs spend their time foraging on the ocean floor down to 300 metres deep. They measure up to 3.7 metres from claw tip to claw tip.

Deepest scuba dive

Ahmed Gabr is an Egyptian scuba diver who holds world records for both the deepest scuba dive (male), and the deepest scuba dive in sea water.

TOP OF THE TWILIGHT ZONE

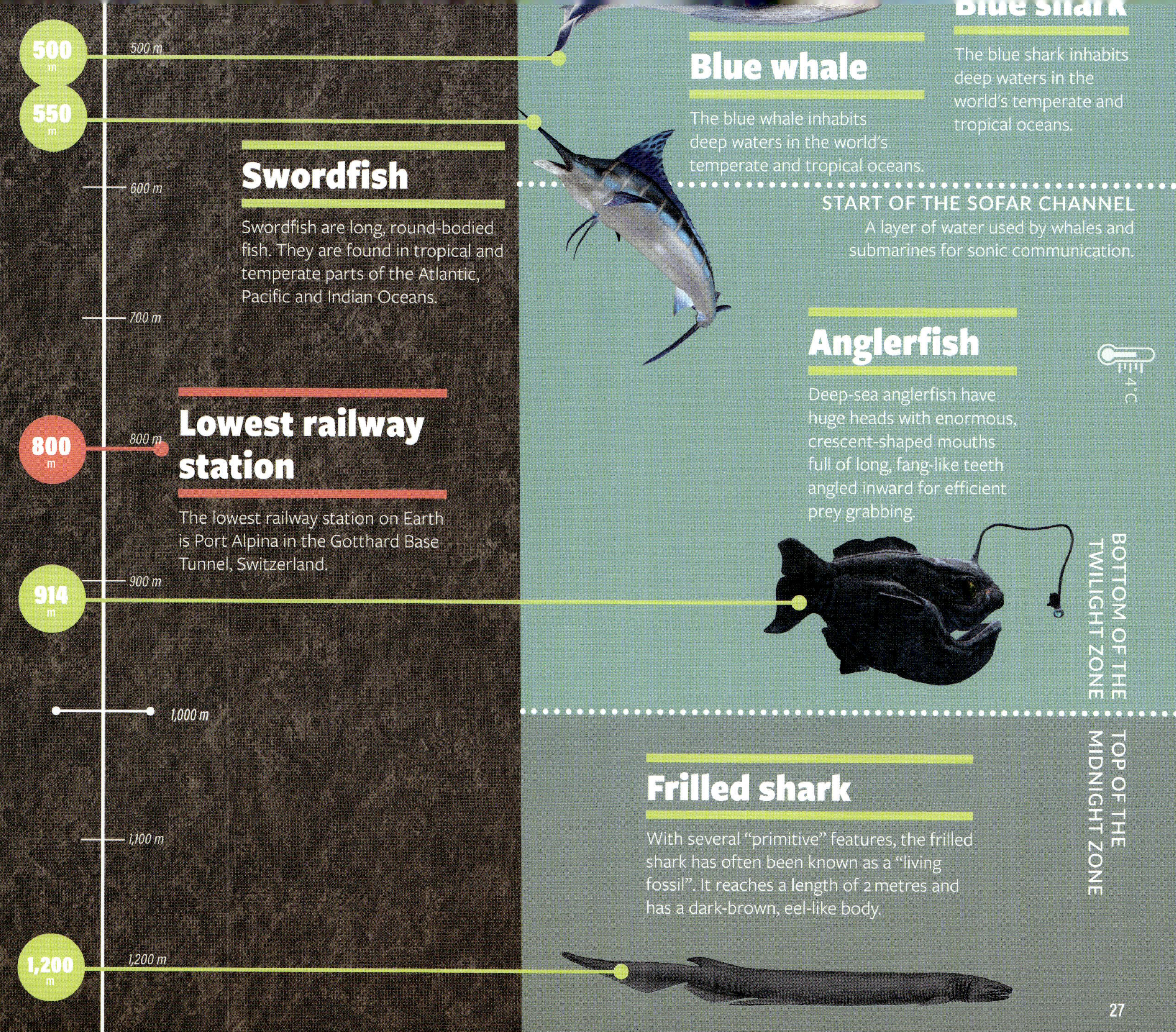

Blue shark

The blue shark inhabits deep waters in the world's temperate and tropical oceans.

Blue whale

The blue whale inhabits deep waters in the world's temperate and tropical oceans.

Swordfish

Swordfish are long, round-bodied fish. They are found in tropical and temperate parts of the Atlantic, Pacific and Indian Oceans.

START OF THE SOFAR CHANNEL

A layer of water used by whales and submarines for sonic communication.

Anglerfish

Deep-sea anglerfish have huge heads with enormous, crescent-shaped mouths full of long, fang-like teeth angled inward for efficient prey grabbing.

Lowest railway station

The lowest railway station on Earth is Port Alpina in the Gotthard Base Tunnel, Switzerland.

BOTTOM OF THE TWILIGHT ZONE

TOP OF THE MIDNIGHT ZONE

Frilled shark

With several "primitive" features, the frilled shark has often been known as a "living fossil". It reaches a length of 2 metres and has a dark-brown, eel-like body.

1,300 m

1,400 m

1,500 m

Deepest coal mine

The Jindrich II mine in the Czech Republic was the deepest coal mine until its closure in 1991.

1,600 m

1,700 m

1,800 m

1,900 m

2,000 m

2,000 m

Giant octopus

The giant Pacific octopus or North Pacific giant octopus is a large marine cephalopod. It is found from the intertidal zone down to depths of 2,000 metres in cold, oxygen-rich water.

2,140 m

2,200 m

2,250 m

2,300 m

2,200 m

2,300 m

2,400 m

2,500 m

2,600 m

2,700 m

2,800 m

2,900 m

Giant isopod

Giant isopods are important scavengers in the deep-sea environment. They are mainly found from the gloomy sublittoral zone at a depth of 170 metres to the darkness of the bathypelagic zone at 2,140 metres.

Yeti crab

Yeti crabs were discovered in 2005 south of Easter Island in the South Pacific, living on vents of warm water at a depth of about 2,200 metres.

Deepest dinosaur fossil

In 2006, an oil rig crew found a dinosaur fossil in the North Sea off the coast of Norway. The fossil has been identified as the knucklebone of a plateosaurus, a massive, plant-eating dinosaur that lived 200 million years ago.

Sperm whale

The sperm whale is the largest toothed predator. Mature males average 16 metres in length. The sperm whale feeds primarily on squid. Plunging to 2,250 metres for prey, it is the second-deepest diving mammal.

3,000 m

3,000 m

3,100 m

3,200 m

3,300 m

3,400 m

3,500 m

3,600 m

Dumbo octopus

This octopus is nicknamed Dumbo because they flap a pair of large ear-like fins to swim, like the cartoon flying elephant. Estimated to be about 2 metres long and and weigh about 6 kg.

Titanic

The *Titanic* was a British passenger liner that sank in the North Atlantic Ocean about 600 km off the coast of Canada. In the early hours of 15 April 1912, the ship hit an iceberg during its maiden voyage from Southampton to New York. More than 1,500 died, making it one of the worst maritime disasters in history. The *Titanic* was the largest ship afloat at the time.

DID YOU KNOW? The wreck of the *Titanic* was discovered in 1985, more than 70 years after the disaster.

Titanic

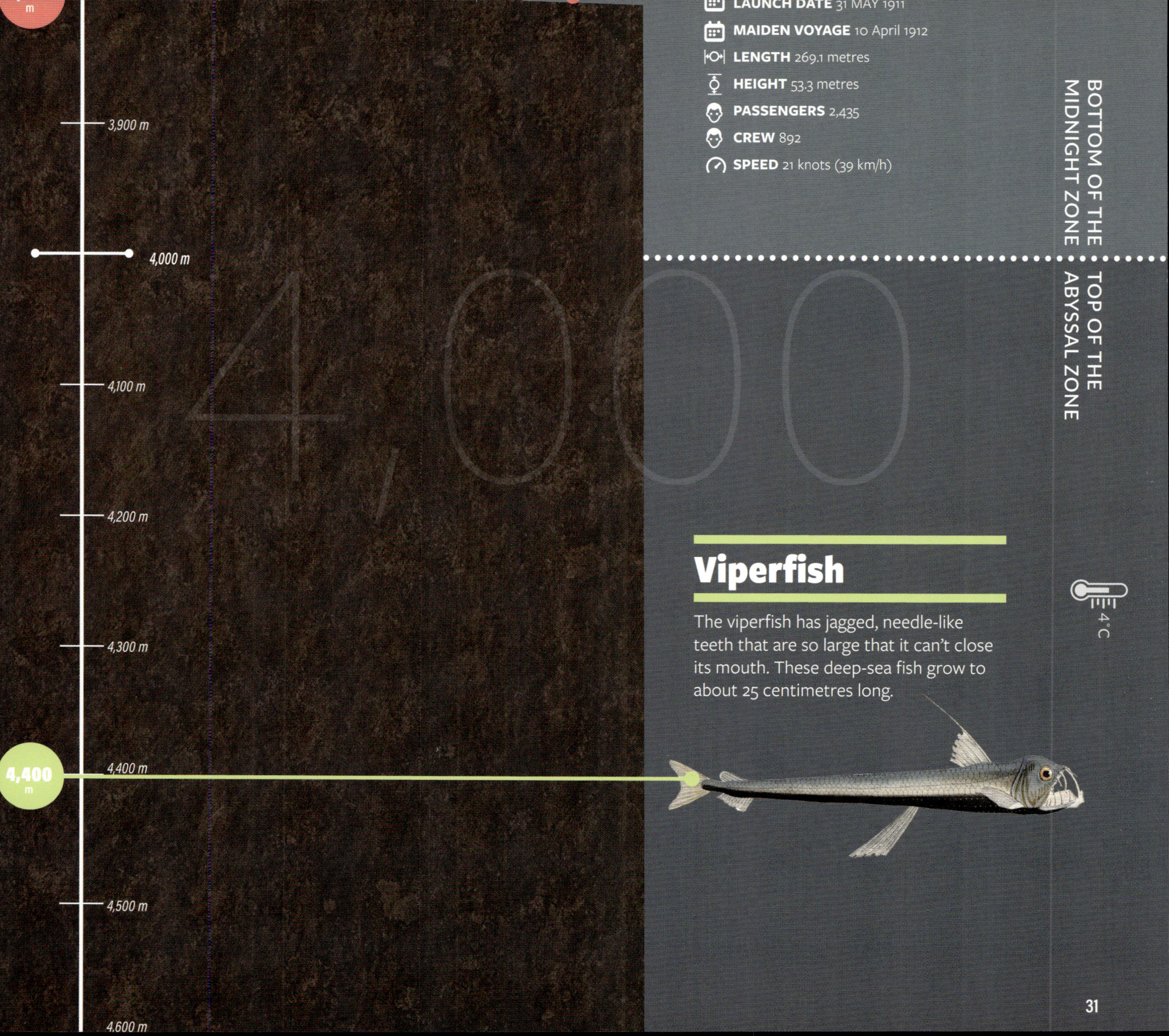

LAUNCH DATE 31 MAY 1911
MAIDEN VOYAGE 10 April 1912
LENGTH 269.1 metres
HEIGHT 53.3 metres
PASSENGERS 2,435
CREW 892
SPEED 21 knots (39 km/h)

Viperfish

The viperfish has jagged, needle-like teeth that are so large that it can't close its mouth. These deep-sea fish grow to about 25 centimetres long.

Fangtooth

The fangtooth is among the deepest living fish. Its normal habitat ranges as high as about 2,000 metres, but it has been found swimming at depths near 5,000 metres. The fangtooth reaches only about 16 centimetres long.

5,500 m

5,600 m

5,700 m

5,760 m

Deepest shipwreck

SS *Rio Grande* was sunk by two US ships in the South Atlantic Ocean in January 1944. It was discovered on 28 November 1996, using sonar technology.

5,800 m

5,900 m

6,000 m

6,100 m

6,200 m

Nautile

The *Nautile* is capable of housing three people. It has still imaging cameras, colour video cameras, and a number of floodlights. It is fitted with two robotic arms to allow remote manipulation. *Nautile* can stay under water for up to 8 hours at a time.

LAUNCH DATE 1984
LENGTH 8 metres
DRAFT 3.81 metres
CREW 3
SPEED 1.5 knots (2.8 km/h)

6,300 m

6,351 m

Closest point on ground to the Earth's centre

The bottom of the Litke Deep is the deepest point of the Arctic Ocean.

6,400 m

6,500 m

6,500 m

DID YOU KNOW? DSV *Alvin* was involved in the exploration of the wreckage of the *Titanic* in 1986.

DSV *Alvin*

DSV *Alvin* is a manned deep-ocean research submersible owned by the United States Navy.

- **LAUNCH DATE** 5 JUNE 1964
- **LENGTH** 7.1 metres
- **HEIGHT** 3.7 metres
- **CREW** 3
- **SPEED** 3.7 km/h

6,600 m

6,700 m

6,800 m

6,900 m

7,000 m

7,200 m
7,300 m
7,400 m
7,500 m
7,600 m
7,700 m
7,800 m
7,900 m

8,000 m

8,100 m

8,145 m

8,200 m

8,300 m

8,400 m

8,500 m

8,600 m

8,648 m

8,700 m

Deepest fish

The hadal snailfish is a species of deep-sea fish. This pale, tadpole-like fish reaches up to 28.8 cm and 160 g in weight, and is found in deep ocean trenches.

Puerto Rico Trench

The Puerto Rico Trench is located on the boundary between the Caribbean Sea and the Atlantic Ocean.

DID YOU KNOW? The Puerto Rico Trench is about 1,750 km long and 100 km wide.

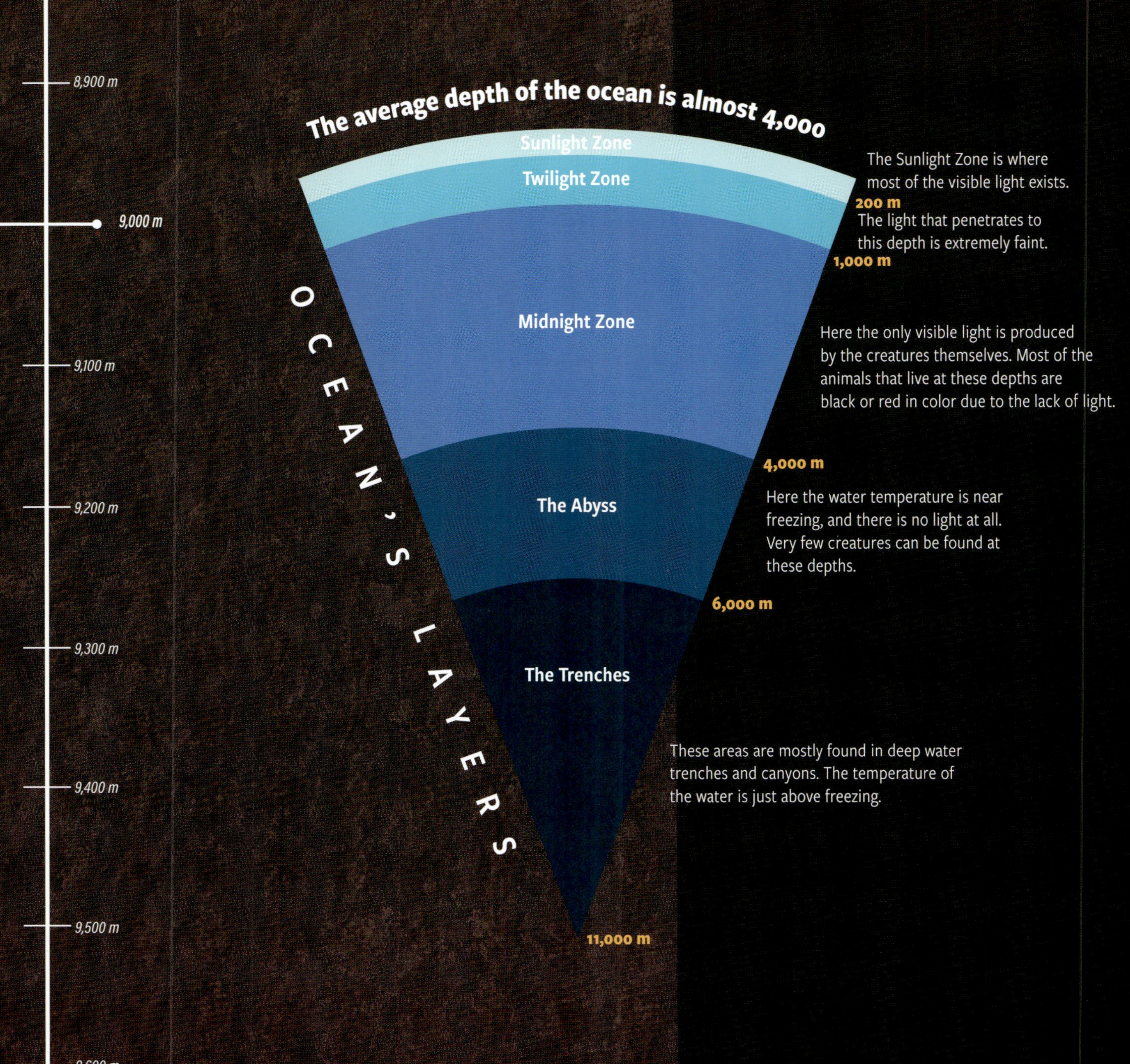
8,900 m
9,000 m
9,100 m
9,200 m
9,300 m
9,400 m
9,500 m
9,600 m
The average depth of the ocean is almost 4,000
OCEAN'S LAYERS
Sunlight Zone
Twilight Zone
Midnight Zone
The Abyss
The Trenches
The Sunlight Zone is where most of the visible light exists.
200 m
The light that penetrates to this depth is extremely faint.
1,000 m
Here the only visible light is produced by the creatures themselves. Most of the animals that live at these depths are black or red in color due to the lack of light.
4,000 m
Here the water temperature is near freezing, and there is no light at all. Very few creatures can be found at these depths.
6,000 m
These areas are mostly found in deep water trenches and canyons. The temperature of the water is just above freezing.
11,000 m

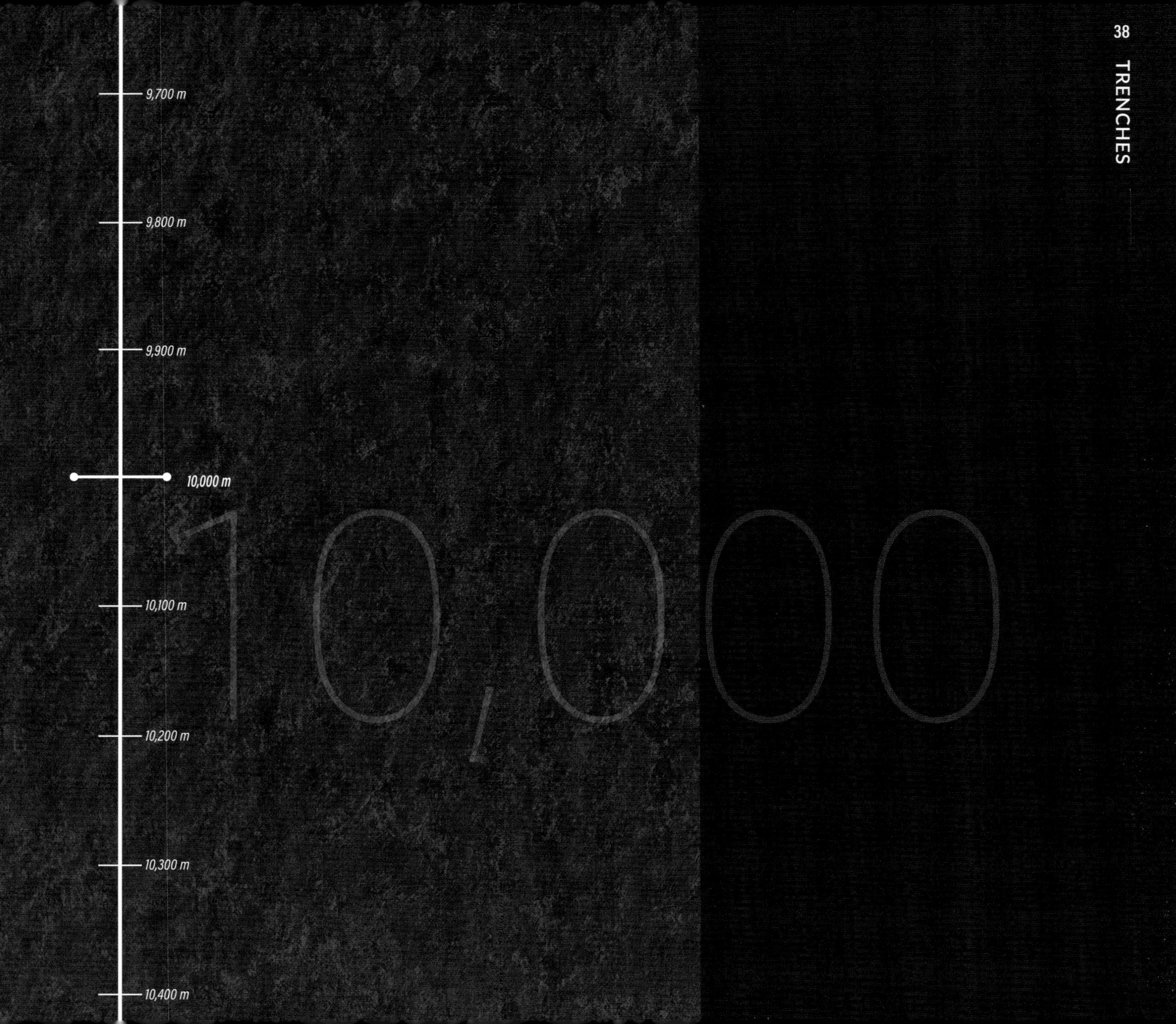
9,700 m
9,800 m
9,900 m
10,000 m
10,000
10,100 m
10,200 m
10,300 m
10,400 m

10,500 m

10,600 m

10,685 m

10,700 m

10,800 m

10,900 m

Change of scale

11,034 m

11,000 m

12,262 m

20,000 m

30,000 m

40,000 m

Deepest oil well

In September 2009, the Deepwater Horizon drilling rig drilled the deepest oil well in history, reaching a depth of 10,685 metres.

Deepest point in ocean

Challenger Deep is a small slot-shaped valley in the Mariana Trench and at a depth of 11,034 metres is the deepest part of the world's oceans. It is located in the western Pacific Ocean, to the east of the Mariana Islands. The Mariana Trench is about 2,550 kms long and 69 kms wide.

Deepest artificial point on Earth

The Kola Superdeep Borehole is the result of a scientific drilling project by the Soviet Union. It took 19 years – from 1970 to 1989 – to drill to 12,262 metres.

Deepsea Challenger

Deepsea Challenger (DCV 1) is a 7.3 metres deep-diving submersible designed to reach the bottom of Challenger Deep.

DID YOU KNOW? The *Deepsea Challenger* was built in Sydney.

BOTTOM OF THE TRENCHES

0-3°C

EARTH'S CRUST

TOP OF THE UPPER MANTLE

BOTTOM OF THE UPPER MANTLE

TOP OF THE LOWER MANTLE

EARTH'S LAYERS

CLASSIFIED BY CHEMICAL COMPOSITION

The Earth can be divided into the crust, upper mantle, lower mantle, outer core, and inner core.

The Earth's mantle is a layer of silicate rock.

In the mantle, temperatures range from around 200°C at the upper boundary to approximately 4,000°C at the core-mantle boundary.

The outer core of the Earth is a fluid layer composed of iron and nickel.

The Earth's inner core is a solid ball, which was first discovered by Inge Lehmann in 1936. It has a radius of about 1,220 kilometres and is composed of an iron-nickel alloy. The temperature at the surface of the inner core is approximately 5,430°C, which is the temperature at the surface of the Sun.

50,000 m
60,000 m
70,000 m
80,000 m
90,000 m
Change of scale
1,000,000 m
2,000,000 m

BOTTOM OF THE LOWER MANTLE

THE OUTER CORE

THE INNER CORE

3,000,000 m

4,000,000 m

DID YOU KNOW? The inner core is as hot as the Sun's surface!

5,000,000 m

You have reached the centre of the Earth!

6,000,000 m

6,371,000 m The Earth's inner core is a solid ball with a radius of about 1,220 kms. It is composed of an iron–nickel alloy. The temperature at the inner core's surface is estimated to be approximately 5,430°C, about the same temperature at the surface of the Sun.

Index

Glossary

Absorb Take in or soak up

Aerodynamic Able to move through air in a smooth and fast way

Alloy Metal made by combining two or more metals

Altitude Height above sea level of a place or thing

Amateur Someone who does something because they enjoy it rather than as a job

Antenna A device by which signals such as radio waves are received or sent

Arthropod An invertebrate animal with a segmented body, such as an insect, spider or crustacean

Artificial Made by people; not occurring naturally

Ascent To climb upwards

Atmosphere The air around the Earth or around another planet

Atomic Using the energy produced by splitting atoms

Autonomous Independent, has the power to govern itself

Bathypelagic Living creatures that inhabit ocean depths of between 1,000 and 3,000 metres

Boundary Where something ends and something else begins; the limit of an area

Cargo Goods carried by ship, plane, train or truck

Cephalopod A mollusc such as an octopus or squid

Colony A community of animals or plants living close together or forming a physically connected structure

Commercial Making or intending to make a profit

Composition Putting various elements together; formation

Constituent A part or component of something

Core Central part

Cosmonaut Russian astronaut

Crescent A single curve, broad in the centre and tapering at each end

Crust A hardened layer or coating on the surface of something

Cylinder An object shaped like a wide tube

Dense A dense substance is very heavy in relation to its size

Descent The act of moving to a lower place or position

Diameter The length of a straight line crossing the centre of a circle

Domesticated Adapted over time to live with humans in a domestic setting

Dwelling A shelter where people live, such as a house

Efficient Producing desired results with little or no waste

Elevation Height

Elliptical Having an oval shape

Engineer A person who designs and builds

Environment The circumstances and conditions by which one is surrounded

Evidence A sign or indication

Extinct No longer active

Foraging Searching for food

Fossil A remnant preserved from a past geological age

Freediving Diving underwater without breathing apparatus

Gravity The force that attracts one body to another body of significantly greater mass

Habitat A place or environment where a plant or animal naturally lives

Hazardous Exposing one to risk

Inhabit Live in

Inland The internal part of the country, not the coast

Interspersed Inserted at intervals

Intertidal zone The area of the seashore which is covered at high tide and uncovered at low tide

Isopod A type of crustacean

Jagged A sharply uneven edge or surface

Knots A unit of speed, used to measure the movement of ships, aircrafts and wind

Laden Carrying a load or burden

Latitude Distance north or south from the Equator